Thank You

The Day I Met Bob

A 5 Year Old's Introduction To Goals

Destin Gregory **with** Eric Gregory

ISBN: 0692678271
ISBN-13: 978-0692678275

DESTIN GREGORY

DEDICATION

We dedicate this production to each other. With a continuous flow of love and creativity, we continue to make it happen. Our teamwork can't be beat.

Having each other is all we need, but we are blessed with an abundance in all we will ever want.

Eric & Destin Gregory

ACKNOWLEDGMENTS

We first and foremost would like to acknowledge Mr. Bob Proctor. Your consistent lessons of wisdom, and your willingness to share them with the world, has led to this milestone of a moment with us. We greatly appreciate the amazing work that you do and the precious part you have played in making this production a success. Thank you Bob, sincerely.

We would also like to acknowledge our loving and supportive friends and family who multiplied our efforts in bringing this wonderful story to the world. Thank you, thank you, thank you.

And lastly, we would like to give a very special "Thank You" to **New Day Services** including the entire staff. Your encouragement, support, and generosity has been greatly appreciated. You guys provide empowering services that will benefit generation after generation. We are blessed to have you as a partner in our growth.

DESTIN GREGORY

Me, My Dad, and Bob
(introduction)

Hi, my name is Destin and I'm telling the wonderful story of when I, as a little five year old, met Bob Proctor. I'm sure that you will enjoy this story. This is a true tale that's fun and full of useful ideas that can help you succeed in anything you want to do.

I know you may be wondering what such a young kid could know about Mr. Bob Proctor, or even how I could know of this world famous man. I'll just say this, Bob is a very cool old man who teaches people how to set goals and use their minds to be happy and <u>successful</u>.

And he knows how to make a lot of money! I really should say, "earn a lot of money", because the only people who "make money" are the people who print it at the factory. This is also one of Mr. Proctor's cool lessons.

I know these awesome things about Bob because of my awesome Dad. My dad loves to study and learn from Mr. Proctor. And my Dad is actually helping me tell this story.

My Dad often tells me that even though he is not in school anymore, he will always have teachers. His teachers can be anyone who knows something that he wants to learn for himself. And the coolest part is that he gets to pick his teachers. I would love to be able to do that at my school!

My Dad has other great people that he looks up to as well, but Mr. Bob Proctor is really his favorite. And the things I have learned so far about Bob makes him a favorite to me as well.

I invite you all to join me as I share our amazing story of how I was introduced to the wonderful idea of goals, and then to Mr. Bob Proctor.

THE MAN IN THE SPEAKERS

As far back as I can remember my Dad has always had some strange man talking through the speakers.

He'd be talking through the speakers while I was riding in the car. I'd hear him while my Dad was getting me ready for school. Sometimes I would even hear the man talking while my Dad was in the bathroom.

My Dad must have really liked that man!

One day, while riding home from school, I heard the man say my name, "... Destin for greatness..."

"Dad! Dad! He just said my name." I shouted with

excitement.

My Dad laughed and said, " That's right son, but he said destin-ed, destined for greatness. Do you know what that means?" he asked me.

"No sir, what does it mean?" I replied

"It's when someone will be great at something no matter what. They are destined to be great. They are Destin-ed for greatness." He told me, making sure that I heard my name again.

"Oh… so I'm destined for greatness?" I asked hoping that I was.

"You got that right son. And you can be or do anything that you put your mind to." My Dad said with a big grin.

I sat back into my booster seat smiling from ear to ear. After a while, I asked my Dad the name of the man talking through the speakers. He told me.

And that was the day I became <u>interested</u> in Mr. Bob Proctor.

Gooooaaals!

Now that I knew a little more about the man talking through the speakers, I started to pay more attention to what he was saying.

I began to notice that Mr. Proctor said a few words a lot. "Goals", "Faith", and "Success" were some of the words he would say again and again.

And he always talked about thinking and using our imaginations. I can remember one of my favorite cartoons saying the same thing, "You gotta sit in the chair and think, think, thi-iii-ink." I loved that blue dog.

My Dad was always around to explain anything when I would ask. He told me about goals and how important they are to growing and getting better and better at something.

I was a little <u>confused</u> at first, so to better understand I asked, "Goals? But we make goals on my soccer team. That's not the same thing is it?"

"Well, not exactly son." my Dad said with a chuckle. "The goals for your soccer team are points just like touchdowns are in football. The goals we are talking about can be anything that we want for ourselves." He answered.

"Anything?" I asked.

"Anything son. As long as it is good and for the better. And definitely something that you will be proud of." he told me.

I thought about that for a moment then said with excitement, " I want to make some goals for myself!"

"Then let's do it son!" my Dad said with a cheer. "I'll help you come up with two good ones, then I will show you a list of some goals I'm working on."

I was excited as I began to think of some good goals for myself. The first thing that came to my mind was my soccer team, the Mighty Jaguars, and how cool it would be to score three goals in one game.

I'm a pretty good soccer player, but I had never scored three points in one game. I knew it would be tough and take a lot of practice, but I made it my first goal anyway.

My Dad told me that Bob teaches us to set big goals that may even be scary to us. But as long as we believe, have faith, and only think of ways it can be done, we can make it happen.

I let my Dad help me pick my second goal. It was to get a good behavior mark from my teacher every day for two weeks in a row.

This goal would really be hard because I get a little impatient at the end of the school day and sometimes act out. But I was happy with this goal too because it would make me a better student, and my Dad promised me a new toy if I could do it. So I took on the <u>challenge</u>.

After writing out my goals and sticking them on the wall in my room, my Dad showed me his list of goals he wanted to <u>accomplish</u>. One goal was to sell five cars in one day at his job. Another goal was to learn how to speak Spanish. He even had a goal to be the best Dad in the world. He called it his <u>Ultimate</u> Father goal. I thought that was very cool.

But there was one other goal that really stuck out to me. My Dad had set a goal to meet and study with Bob Proctor, wow! I knew how much my Dad enjoyed learning from Mr. Proctor, but I never thought that he would actually meet him.

Thinking of all the cool videos I had seen of Bob and <u>imagining</u> my own Dad being next to him, I said to my Dad with excitement, "Promise me that you'll bring me with you to meet Mr. Proctor. Promise! Promise!"

"I'm sure we can make that happen son. I promise I won't go to meet him without you. In fact, I believe he would even like to meet you as well." he told me with <u>confidence.</u>

Now I was really beginning to like goals. I was learning from my Dad that you can just sit back and think of what you want, write it down, and then decide to make it happen. It felt like I was learning a superpower or something.

I told my Dad that I really hoped he got his goals,

and he told me the same. After that he started playing

Bob Proctor again.

THE DAY I MET BOB

SUCCESS ON SUCCESS

Some time had passed now, and yup, I completed both of my goals!

On our second to last match of the season, I scored three goals and played my best game ever. Everyone cheered for me. The feeling was incredible.

My good behavior goal went great as well. Not only did I go two straight weeks getting good marks, but I continued getting good marks for another week. And I'm learning to settle down more while waiting to get out of school.

My Dad was very proud of my success. We went out and celebrated at my favorite eating place after my record breaking soccer match. And for my great behavior in school, I got a cool new video game.

I understood what my Dad had told me about goals, but I never knew it would feel this good. I was very proud of myself.

One night, while getting me ready for bed, my Dad told me he had a great big surprise for me. He acted like he wouldn't tell me, but he knew I would keep bugging him about it until I fell asleep.

"What is it? What is it?", I asked over and over again. "Please tell me Dad."

My Dad gave in, "Okay son. Remember one of the big goals I've been working on? The one you made me promise to have you with me when I accomplished it?"

I thought for a while, then my eyes grew wide. "Bob Proctor!", I said, not sleepy anymore. "We're going to meet Bob!"

"That's right son!" my Dad said with a huge smile. He seemed to be even more excited than I was. "In just two short weeks we will be on our way to meet and learn even more from the great Bob Proctor. We did it son!"

He told me that we wouldn't just be meeting him, but we would be spending a whole weekend with him. Wow, a whole weekend with Mr. Proctor would be wonderful. I thought of what he would look like in person. I thought of what I would say. I thought of how my Dad would finally accomplish his goal.

"Good job Dad", I said to him. He kissed my head goodnight, said thanks, and wished me <u>successful</u> dreams.

THE DAY I MET BOB

THE BIG LET DOWN

The two weeks had finally passed and our special weekend was here. My Dad was so excited that he changed his clothes three times before he decided on what he would wear.

He told me that he really wanted to make a good first <u>impression</u> on Mr. Proctor. Of course, I didn't know what a "good first impression" was, but it had to be important so I asked, "What's a good first impression Dad?"

"Well first of all son, a first impression is simply the way you make someone think or feel about you after you first meet or speak with them. You can make a good impression or a bad impression. But remember that you'll always leave an impression behind wherever you go." he told me.

"Well I want to leave a good first impression too. We're meeting Bob Proctor, we have to make sure he likes us." I replied.

Now we were all geared up and headed to see Mr. Proctor. I could see all of the happiness and excitement on my Dad's face. Just looking at him made me excited too. He had on his favorite dress shirt and was wearing the cool slip-on shoes he hardly ever wore. Boy was he ready!

We finally made it to our destination. It was a great big building with several other big buildings surrounding it. It looked like a castle or something! Everything was shiny and looked brand new.

There was a big water park with big slides and diving boards. There were cool statues of men and women, and great big colorful water fountains. This place was incredible.

"Wow. Is this where Bob lives?" I asked in amazement.

"No son, I'm afraid not." my Dad chuckled. "This place is called a resort hotel. Everything here is the best of the best. From the food to the fun, anything you get here will be the best you can get."

Still in amazement I said, "This place is amazing. We barely got here and this place is already making a good first impression on me."

"You're silly son", my Dad laughed as we found a good parking spot. "Now let me go see if I can get you in so that you'll really be impressed." Then he went inside.

My Dad had the babysitter, Ms. Jenny, drive us just in case I couldn't stay. He had told me that he would have to check and make sure it would be okay for me to stay with him. There would be only adults here, and a five year old could be a <u>distraction.</u>

I hoped everything would be alright. I really wanted to see Mr. Proctor in person, and be with my Dad while he got his goal.

Just as I was thinking that, I saw my Dad hurrying back to the car, "Can I come in Dad? Can I?", I shouted out to him. As he came closer I could see the <u>disappointing</u> look on his face.

"I'm afraid not son." he said sadly. "I asked someone who worked with Bob and he said that you have to be at least 12 years old to come in. I'm so sorry son."

I was crushed, but I tried to stay <u>positive</u> like my Dad would. "That's okay Dad." I said trying to hide my disappointment. "At least we tried."

"I know son, but you know what? We're going to do more than try. We're going to *make* it happen. Even Mr. Proctor teaches us to never give up. So I'm going to figure out something for us.", he said. "Just watch son, I got you."

I could tell that he was serious. And I knew he would find a way. I was sad because of not being able to stay with my Dad, but I felt better knowing that he would be working to get me in there with him. If anybody could do it, he could. And I believed he would.

There happened to be a festival in town near the resort hotel. My Dad asked Ms. Jenny to take me to the festival while we waited on him to finish his first evening with Mr. Proctor.

My evening got a lot better after that. There were cool rides and fun games everywhere. I had a blast! But even with all the fun at the festival I still

wondered how my Dad was doing with Mr. Proctor.
I couldn't wait to find out.

THERE'S NO QUITTING ON GOALS

The next morning I was gently shaken awoke by my Dad. We had made it home a little late the night before, and with all the fun at the festival, I fell fast asleep on the ride home.

I was still very sleepy when my dad woke me up, and it seemed to be very early. As I rubbed my eyes to see more clearly I could see that my Dad was already dressed and ready to leave the house.

"Destin... Destin... are you awake?" He asked, shaking me a few more times." Well I'm off to meet with Mr. Proctor again. We're meeting early today."

I tried to speak clearly but my morning voice cracked with each word. "Am I able to come with you today?" I asked.

"I still haven't found a way son, but don't worry. We still have one day left and I am <u>determined</u> to do everything in my power to get you and me in front of Mr. Proctor together. I promise son, okay?

"Okay Dad." I said back to him.

"Ms. Jenny is on her way to look after you while I'm gone. She should be here any second now. You go ahead and get back to sleep. I love you, and I'll see

THE DAY I MET BOB

you soon." he told me. He gave me the forehead kiss and left the room.

I was back to sleep in seconds.

———————

It seemed like it took forever for my Dad to get back home that day, but as soon as he arrived my name was the first thing out of his mouth. "Destin! Destin! Where are you?" he shouted playfully as he closed the door behind him.

"Hey Dad, what's up?" I said rushing toward him.

"How would you like to have lunch with Bob Proctor tomorrow?" My Dad asked with excitement.

"Are you for real, Dad?" I asked, hoping he wasn't kidding me. He nodded his head with a great big smile. "Yay! That would be perfect. I knew you would do it Dad, you're the best."

"No, you the best son." he said back. Then he rushed toward me to scoop me up onto his shoulders and began twirling me around in circles.

Boy was I happy. Even though it seemed like I wouldn't be able to meet Mr. Proctor, I never stopped believing that it could happen. My Dad always tells me that whenever you still have a chance, no matter how small, never give up. You'll never know how close you were if you give up.

After my head stopped spinning from all the circles we did I ran off to my room. "Wait, where are you going? my Dad asked.

"I have to pick out my clothes for our lunch tomorrow." I said to him like he should have already known. "I'm going to make the best first impression on Mr. Proctor. I can't wait!"

Head Up and Chest Out

I went to sleep early that night just so the next day would come faster. I was so excited the next morning that my Dad barely had to say my name to wake me. And it didn't take long to get me dressed and ready either. I had took a bath and laid out my clothes perfectly the night before.

I had on my favorite button down dress shirt, my classic designer blue jeans, and my cool brown cowboy boots. I was looking mighty good. My Dad even let me wear my gold necklace and watch that I only wore for special days. Well this day was special, and I was feeling pretty special too.

We finally arrived at the beautiful resort hotel. The place was just as amazing as I remembered, and this time I was going in. It wasn't quite lunchtime yet, but my Dad said it would be ok for me to come in and hang out until it was time.

When I walked into the hotel I felt like I was entering a theme park for grown-ups. Everything was amazing. The floors were so shiny, and the ceiling was so high. There were great big trees and plants and even waterfalls on the inside. And the people who worked there were very polite and happy.

My Dad still had his morning meeting to go to. As Ms. Jenny and I were still looking around in amazement, my Dad stopped one of the workers in uniform to speak to her, "Excuse me ma'am, I'm here with Bob Proctor. I just wanted to know if there was an area where my guest could wait for me until lunch."

The nice lady smiled and said, "Sure thing, sir. They can wait here in our lobby area with no problem." Then the lady turned to looked at me, smiled and said, "Or better yet, I would be happy to take them on a full tour of our 5 star resort hotel while they're waiting."

"That would be wonderful.", my Dad said thankfully. "Thank you so much."

Then my Dad told me that he would see me in a bit and then he rushed off to get to his meeting. The day was already starting off great. I waited with Ms. Jenny in the lobby for a little while before the happy lady in the uniform came to take us to see the rest of the hotel.

By the end of our tour I really felt like I was in a castle. It seemed like this was the place of someone's dreams. There were swimming pools on the inside. They had a game room with all the new games and unlimited tokens. They even had a river of water that flowed through a restaurant. And that was just half of the hotel. I remember thinking, "I can really see myself living in a place like this."

It was almost lunchtime so we headed back to the lobby to wait on my Dad. He was already there waiting on me. "Hey son. Did you have fun on the tour?" he ask me.

"Yes sir! They have a swimming pool on the inside and a game room where I played all the games." I said with excitement. "Is it time to meet Mr. Proctor now?"

With a big grin he said, "Yes it is, my boy. I just wanted to talk with you before we went in. Now, it took a lot for us to get this point. Even when it seemed like it wouldn't happen we kept the faith and didn't stop trying. And that's what I want to talk to you about son, Faith." he said, serious now.

"When we walk in there I want you to walk like you belong in the room, with your head up and chest out. That's what faith is, believing that your goal is already accomplished. So do you got the faith?" he asked me.

"Yes I do!" I said with confidence.

"Well let's go then." he replied. Then off we went, walking like we owned the place.

THE DAY I MET BOB

The New Kid at Lunch

As we got closer to the entrance of the big lunch room I began to see a lot of grown-ups with badges around their necks like my Dad's. This must be it, I thought as I began to get a little scared.

The grown-ups were too busy talking to each other to really notice me, so I made it to the entrance without much attention. As soon as we walked into the lunchroom that all changed. It seemed like everyone stopped what they were doing and just looked at me.

I felt so small and a little scared, but I remembered my Dad's words then held my head up and poked my little chest out. I had to keep my faith going. I belonged here.

My Dad led us to our table where we would be eating. There were others at our table and none of them looked like Bob Proctor, so I asked, "Dad? I thought we were eating with Mr. Proctor. Who are these people?"

Laughing, my Dad said, "I'm sorry son. These nice people are here like me to see and learn from Bob. This is called a V.I.P. lunch where if you have a V.I.P. badge, like this one, you can have lunch here with Mr. Proctor and ask him questions while we eat."

"Oh, okay." I said, still a little nervous.

"Just relax son." my Dad said rubbing my back. "Our time with Mr. Proctor is coming soon. Oh, and look, here comes our lunch. I think you're going to like it very much."

When I looked over I seen about 10 hotel workers, in the same uniform as the nice tour lady, carrying plates of steaming food on big silver trays. One of them came to our table and began putting the plates down.

The food looked like it was torn out of a cooking book or something. Everything looked picture perfect. We had salmon fish, green vegetables called asparagus, steaming white rice, and a few other foods that I didn't know the name for.

I love fish and seafood so I went for the salmon, and boy was it good. I must have been more hungry than I was nervous because I ate that salmon fish like I was in my own school's cafeteria.

While I was eating Mr. Proctor had entered the room and took his seat at the front by the stage. My Dad pointed him out to me, and I thought he looked just like he did in the videos.

Mr. Proctor looked super clean in his blue suit and silky blue tie. His white hair was slicked back and combed perfectly. He was an old man, but he was a cool old man with style. Me and my friends call it "swag", and Mr. Proctor definitely had it.

"Are we going to get a chance to ask Bob some

questions today?" I asked my Dad.

"Well I had a chance to write my question down on a card at yesterday's lunch. I couldn't think of anything to ask him. So you know what I did?" he asked with a grin.

"What Dad, what did you do?" I replied, knowing he was up to something.

"I wrote and told him how you know of him and how bad you wanted to be here with me to meet him. And then I asked if I could bring you to today's lunch because you didn't want him to get too old before you could meet him." my Dad told me.

I couldn't believe it. "Well, what did he say?" I asked quickly.

"I didn't turn it in in time for him to read it yesterday. But I did talk to the pretty lady who collected the cards and told her how important my question was. She promised that she would put it first in line for today's lunch. So we're about to see…" said my Dad, rubbing his hands together.

"Well what if she didn't do it or forgot or something." I asked, not wanting to leave our goal in someone else's hands.

"That's where your faith comes in son." he said back to me. "For the things that we can't control, we have to use our faith. You still got your faith, right?" I nodded and started to smile again. "Well head up and chest out. Our goal is here."

The Big Stage

As everyone was eating and chatting, Mr. Proctor walked up and sat in his chair on the stage. He cheerfully greeted everyone and hoped we all were enjoying the food. I don't think he noticed me yet, so he just kept on with what he was saying.

And then I heard him say, "And now back to the questions from yesterday…" This was it. This was the moment when he would either read my Dad's card, or not. My Dad looked at me and gave me a wink and a smile then held my hand.

Mr. Proctor continued, "Okay, let's see here. This one is from Eric Gregory and it reads:

'I'm here from Fort Worth and I am writing this on behalf of my son, Destin. He is five years old and have been watching me study you since he was three. He thinks you're a cool old man and was crushed when he learned that he wouldn't be able to attend the seminar with me. He thinks that you will be too old to meet later, and my question is: May my son attend the lunch with me tomorrow to meet you? Thank you.'"

He read it! He read it! I was nervous and excited at the same time as I waited on what he would say next. He said a funny joke about his age that got everyone laughing. Then he looked to the pretty lady who collected the cards and said, "These are yesterday's questions, right? Well I don't think he would have brought his son to-"

At that moment my Dad stood up like a rocket with his hand raised shouting, "Here we are! We're here!"

Mr. Proctor noticed us, smiled, and happily invited us to come on up to the stage. Everyone in the lunchroom turned their attention to us and began to clap and cheer us on.

Walking toward the stage I could hear my heartbeat with each step. But the wonderful feeling of having everyone cheer for me, and seeing Bob standing there with open arms, kept me going.

As my Dad and I reached the stage Mr. Proctor picked me up to sit in his chair facing everyone. He greeted my Dad with a smile and a handshake and then turned to me. He said hello, asked me my name, and then he asked me something else.

"Would you like to sit up here with me in my chair and help me read the rest of the questions?" Mr. Proctor asked with a smile.

I thought about it for a second, looked at all of the grown-ups looking back at me, and slowly shook my head no. I wasn't ready for all of that. Then my Dad stepped in saying, "Remember what Mr. Proctor teaches us: when something good seems a bit scary, we grow by doing it anyway. So what do you say, son?"

My answer was still no. I just wasn't ready to be in front of so many grown-ups trying to help Bob Proctor read. I was just learning to read for myself, and I didn't want to mess anything up. I hoped that I wasn't letting my Dad down by not doing it.

"That's okay son. You did a great job just walking up here with me. That took a lot of <u>courage</u>. I'm very proud of you.", my Dad said. "Now tell Mr. Proctor thank you so we can head back to our seats."

I told Mr. Proctor thanks and he gave me a big hug. Everyone stood up and clapped their hands as we walked back down the stage.

My Dad just couldn't stop smiling. He even high-fived one of the grown-ups on the way back. I could tell that he was feeling really good.

"We did it son! That was the coolest." my Dad whispered loudly as we sat back down. "I am so proud of you."

THE DAY I MET BOB

Success + Reward= Big Fun!

I was happy to make my Dad proud in such a special moment, but I was also very proud of him too. He accomplished his goal and also kept his promise to me. He really showed me what becoming your goal is all about.

I stayed with my Dad for the rest of the lunch listening to Mr. Proctor answer everyone's questions. Everyone had nice things to say to me and my Dad. By then, I was feeling like one of the grown-ups. Head up and chest out.

After finishing our wonderful time with Mr. Proctor, I asked if we could do something to celebrate my Dad's success. My Dad remembered that it was the last day for the town festival and quickly decided that we would be going.

Yes! This was turning out to be the best day ever. Accomplishing goals just make you feel so good. And my Dad said that you should always reward yourself after your success. How can you not love that?

After riding a few rides at the festival my Dad asked me, "Hey, why didn't you want to sit with Mr. Proctor for the rest of the lunch?"

I was a little surprised by his question, but I answered, "I thought it was just going to be you, me, and Bob having lunch. I didn't know all those adults would be there."

"Oh, I see. You wanted a private lunch with Mr. Proctor. You would have been more comfortable then huh?", my Dad said.

"Yes sir." I shot back.

"You know, that's not a bad idea. Our own private lunch with Bob Proctor.", he said thinking. "Are you thinking what I'm thinking, son?"

"I think we should make that our new Proctor goal!" I said with excitement.

"I think you're right.", he said back.

We finished the rest of our evening eating carnival foods, having fun, feeling very successful.

Boy, do I love goals!

Thanks for letting me share my wonderful story with you. If you're anything like me or my Dad, I know you loved it just as much as we loved sharing it.

Destin Gregory

The End

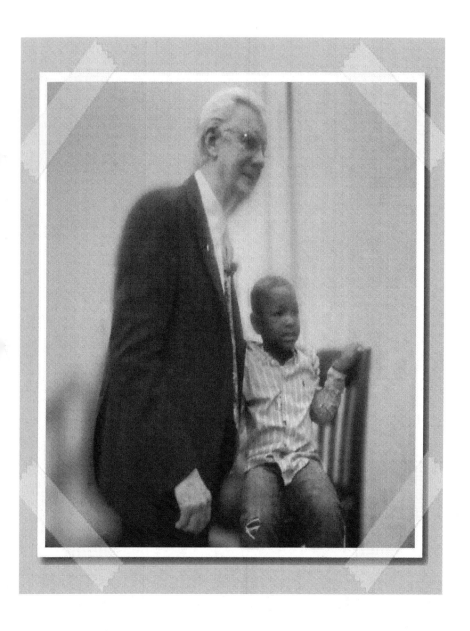

A Message From Dad

Wow, what a good feeling that was. That was a day that I will never forget. It was one of those days when absolutely everything goes perfect.

Meeting and interacting with Bob was an experience more wonderful than I could have expected. But I am more impressed with the fact that my son got to fully participate in the accomplishment of this goal.

I learned a lot in reaching this goal with my son. There were times when it looked like it wouldn't happen, but I kept my faith, and made sure he had his. And I only thought of ways it could work, and it did. I try to keep it that simple.

Keeping your faith going strong and never giving up are the two big lessons I wanted to show my son. It's never too early or too late to learn about goals and how to make them happen.

I'm sure we all think we have some kind of goal we're working on, but usually that goal was set by someone else. It's great to have someone wanting you to be better. But always remember, it's the goals that we set for ourselves that are the most important and will give the most happiness.

So I encourage everyone reading this to set two goals for themselves, write them down in the back of your book, then make up your mind to accomplish them. Take time to think about them often. And only think of ways it can happen.

I promise, once you make it happen, the feeling will be incredible. Remember a goal can be anything you want for yourself that is good and will make you proud. And don't be afraid to think up a big goal. Bob says, "If you think you're thinking big, you're not thinking big enough." I love that line!

Abundance is unlimited. Surprise yourself. You can do it. Thanks for Reading.

Eric Gregory

<u>Glossary</u>

Accomplish- to complete something successfully.

Challenge- a test of yourself that requires special effort.

Confidence- total belief in yourself.

Confused- being unable to think clearly. Not having a full understanding of something.

Courage- the ability to do something even when it scares you.

Determined- having made a firm decision and sticking to it.

<u>Disappointing</u>- being let down. Not getting what was hoped for.

<u>Distraction</u>- a thing that takes your attention away from what needs to be focused on.

<u>Faith</u>- a complete confidence or trust in something even when there is no proof.

<u>Goal-</u> the new idea or desire that will make your life better or more enjoyable.

<u>Imagining</u>- to make pictures in the mind.

<u>Impression</u>- an idea, feeling, or opinion about something or someone.

<u>Interest</u>- something that calls your attention to it.

Positive- anything that is for the good or better

Success- moving toward or completing a goal or purpose.

Ultimate- the best possible or imaginable of its kind

<u>GOALS</u>

<u>GOALS</u>

Going After Goals!

The Big Ones...

Book Series Coming Soon!
follow us
FB Page- @goingaftergoals

Made in the USA
Columbia, SC
27 November 2017